BE STRONG, My Brotha

An Inspirational Guide to Advancing Past Adversity and Chasing Success

DAMIEN O. JEFFERSON

www.sandjempowers.com/publishing/

ISBN-13: 978-0-578-53059-8

ISBN-10: 0-578-53059-7

Publisher: S & J Publishing

DEDICATION

This book is dedicated to my daughter, Janelle Elise Jefferson. Since her conception, I've been in constant growth and have sought innovative ways to improve my leadership abilities. Being a father propelled me into being a greater man and I am grateful for you, Janelle, the wonderful memories, and the sunshine that you have brought into my life. As time continues to pass, I look forward to watching you blossom into the beautiful princess that you are. Daddy loves you, Babygirl.

CONTENTS

INTRODUCTION

Over the course of my life, I have met some great men who've provided me with so much knowledge and wisdom--it is my desire to share it with the next man. As a young boy, I always spent time with my father and his friends on weekends and during weekdays after school hours. I enjoyed the bonds and conversations these men shared with me and, as I grew up, those lessons became clearer and very informative. The men in my life have always motivated and supported me in all my endeavors. I want to take this opportunity to pay it forward with this book. This book is designed to uplift and encourage every Black man--even if the world does not see him as important. It does not matter what position you are in life; I hope that you can gain some insight and develop a sense of empowerment from the jewels presented within the chapters of this book.

The negative notions towards the Black man should really cease and desist because they're only creating a false image of who the Black man really is to his family, his friends, and, in many cases, to the Black man himself. If you are someone heavily influenced by the media, then I am sure you know exactly what I mean. The media may consider the Black man to be dangerous, careless, and uneducated, but the reality is: the Black man is a genuine human being. It really is saddening to wake up daily knowing that the world appears to be against you when you are simply fighting for a place in society. It is not an easy message to cope with knowing the system wants to see you fail when your desire is to provide for your family and live a peaceful, successful life. Life and motivations become intensively hard when you've made mistakes in the past and your goal is to rebuild your life one step at a time, yet you are reminded of the person you were and not the man you wish to become. If any of the mentioned scenarios apply to you or not, I only hope that you will feel valued and know that I understand what you may be facing. You are not in this race alone: there is another Black man rooting for you.

CHAPTER ONE

A Born Winner

Every man was born with a specific purpose for his life as well as gifts to be used in his divine purpose. Some of us knew at a tender age what we wanted to do with our lives, while others may have gone through life searching for that purpose. There are some men that have trouble defining their true identity and purpose because of the way the world has the man on a negative display. To all my brothas, I want you to rise to the occasion because you are a born winner.

Imagine a life where everything was perfect. There was no struggle, no pain, no trial, no error; life was just and fair in pure perfection. Well, wake up: that is not the life of a Black man or anyone else for that matter, but there comes a time where you must realize that you were created to win regardless of your circumstances. Do not be alarmed or dismayed because life does not require you to be perfect; you must be persistent in your efforts to do better and be better. Life requires you to endure the pain, while chasing the goals and dreams that leave you fulfilled and satisfied with your actions. Give yourself a chance and tap into the born winner that lives deep within your mind.

My brotha: take a moment and think about the characteristics of your favorite player(s) on your sports teams. Now ask yourself why is this individual your favorite player. What makes this player different than any other player? At the top of your list of reasoning, I'm sure you're going to say something along the lines of, "He has the attitude of a winner. He's a leader on and off the court. He makes the team better." Now, let's take a moment and define the word *winner.* The Merriam-Webster Dictionary defines a winner as one that wins; one that is successful especially through praiseworthy ability and hard work; a victor especially in games and sports; one that wins admiration; a shot in a court game that is not returned and that scores for the player making it. The Merriam-Webster's English Language Learner definition keeps is simple; it defines *winner* as a very good or successful person or thing. I want you to take a moment to dig deeper and develop the winner deep inside of you.

Source: Merriam-Webster's Collegiate English Dictionary, 2019
Merriam-Webster's English Language Learner, 2019

Now that we have the definition of a winner, we should identify some key components of being a winner. A winner is a leader and takes responsibility for the well-being of the team. Be that winner for your family. Show your family that you take full responsibility for their well-being and will constantly work on improving your abilities as the leader. Brotha: exemplify strength during times of weakness because giving up is the easiest thing to do when times get tough and you start looking rough. Show your family that when life knocks you down, you will get up and keep fighting for the win! Be committed to winning with a heart full of desire and a hunger for more out of life!

Being a winner and a leader shows that you want the best for yourself and your family. Being a winner means that you are committed to creating the necessary opportunities to make your family better; you are setting the foundation and building your family legacy. Listen up, my brotha: not only are you leading by example, but you're also being a supporter for everyone else! This means you commit to always being available for advising; you share your knowledge and wisdom in a supporting manner. Again, the role of a winner is to ensure that everyone succeeds and lives up to their full potential. As the saying goes, "when one wins, we all win," and this should be true and applied to you and your family!

As a winner, you are selfless in your actions and competitive with your endeavors. You are not competing with any other man--only the man you see in the mirror! It would be completely selfish of you to settle for the man that you are instead of striving for the man you were created to be! Don't get lost in the crowd and fade away; stand out, take a shot at life, and proceed to win! The world will try to bring you down. The enemy will try to steal your joy, but you cannot, and I affirm that you will not allow it to happen! You were born to be winners, so do not allow the world or any circumstance to take that away from you.

Principles – W.I.N.N.E.R.

W- Will

Have the will to win in life. Even when you think it's a lose-lose situation, you still win because you get to walk away to fight another day.

I- Integrity

Have integrity with everything that you do. You want people to view you as an honest man--regardless of where you stand in the community.

N- Non-negotiable

Having a winning attitude is non-negotiable. No matter what happens, you will think like a winner, you will act like a winner, and you will live like a winner. No questions asked.

N- Necessary

Being a winner is necessary to progress in life. Do what is required of you, especially when you don't want to because that's when it's needed the most.

E- Engage

Spend time getting engaged to a winning environment. Go connect with other winners and develop a network. Winners support other winners.

R- Read and Research

Study and keep searching for knowledge. You can always learn something new. The more you learn, the more you know; the more you know, the more you grow.

Applying the Lesson

Now that we've determined that you are a winner, it's time to put the lesson into effect. At this time, you are to identify the areas in your life where you are winning and the areas where you need to improve. Make your list as deep and as personal as you would like because you are going to read this list every day for the next month. The purpose for this list is to hold you accountable to be the winner. Accountability is needed when you are determined to improve yourself because the process will not be easy. Trust and believe that there will be times where you want to give up and, at that point, this list will give you the strength to push forward. Okay, I will not hold you any longer--let's get started on your list!

CHAPTER TWO

A Powerful Being

Every man is a born winner and every man has the potential to be a powerful being. When I say powerful being, I'm not talking about the fictional superpowers that our favorite cartoon superheroes possess; the power I am referring to is the power to create and spark a change. I am speaking on the power to rise above the occasion and take charge instead of waiting for someone to say, "Go ahead: you can do it." My brotha, at some point, you should be asking yourself, "Why am I here?", "What am I called to do with my life?", "How can I make a difference?" As you gain the answers to these questions, you'll slowly realize the power within.

In the previous chapter we mentioned your favorite athlete and what it meant to be a winner. Now we are going to discuss what it truly means to be a powerful being.

If you are a fan of the NBA, then you should know of Shaquille O'Neal aka Shaq aka The Diesel. Shaq was a very powerful and dominant center that was a force to be reckoned with deep down in the paint. He made his presence known in every game he played by the way of blocked shots and backboard-breaking dunks. Although he did have a weakness--free throws, Shaq did not dwell on it and did not allow this flaw to keep him from being a powerful player. I say to you, my brotha, do not enable your weaknesses, or shortcomings, to limit you from being a powerful being. Whatever your weaknesses are, you can constantly improve yourself, but you must also have to ambition to it. Understand this: you too have the power to be dominant, confident, and successful in all your endeavors!

I love sports as much as the next man, but you don't have to be a professional athlete to be considered a powerful being. There are guys, such as you those of you reading this book, that have realized they have the potential to be a powerful person and not settling for anything less than extraordinary. I'm talking about guys like worldwide, internationally known speaker, Dr. Eric Thomas, the Hip Hop preacher, who lived in abandoned buildings, got his GED, went to college, and earned his Bachelor's, Master's, and PhD. ET did not allow his past or circumstances to keep him from realizing that he could be a powerful being and have an impact on many lives around him. The only difference between you and Dr. Thomas is he had the willpower to make it happen! Dr. Thomas decided he was going to give his goals 120 percent focus because he wanted to be successful. ET knew where he came from and made it his mission not to go back. Part of being a powerful being is having the courage and willpower to stand up when life's circumstances want you to stay down. Trust and believe that there will be times where you want to give up on life. My brotha, just know there will be moments when you feel the world is coming down on your shoulders, but I'm here to let you know that you are stronger and have power over any problem. Look around in your community and you'll see how possible it is for you to become that business owner, attorney, or powerful person of influence. Don't settle for being powerless like a house without electricity--dig deeper within yourself, develop resurgence in your mentality, and turn on the light switch to being powerful.

When you dwell on the negative, you limit yourself on moving forward and being prosperous. When you grow stagnant in your journey, your negativity may lead to you giving up and feeling powerless. To keep matters simple, think of all the hardships and obstacles you've overcome just to get this far and allow these thoughts to lift you up into a powerful producing state of mind. Challenge yourself to rise and be powerful for your family and your community. Whether you believe it or not, you are building your legacy and I am certain you want to be remembered as being a powerful man who defied the odds placed against him than a man who folded during pressure. My brotha, stand up, dust yourself off, and break those chains because you have the capability to be powerful with your life.

Principles – P.O.W.E.R.

To understand your true power is to understand where you have obtained your power. When you are divinely connected to the power source, you receive the highest voltages in life, no one can steal your powers from you.

P is for perseverance. You grow through the difficult times and gain strength in the midst of it all. You are powerful beyond measure and may not realize it yet.

O stands for optimism. View every trial or disappointment as an opportunity to improve yourself and correct your mistakes. If you fall, get back up, see where you went wrong, and continue the journey.

W is for work. Work on yourself daily. Personal development is a constant process: not an occasional chore that you pick and choose to complete.

E is for enthusiasm. Be excited and embrace the man who you want to become. The man that you are today is only the prototype of the man that you were created to be. A change is going to come, so be glad about it.

R is for reputation. You have the power to revitalize your reputation and grow stronger and righteous with your life.

As you continue to improve and advance, so will your reputation. You will soon be viewed as a man of power and a person of influence. Whatever you do, understand that someone is watching.

Applying the Lesson

Now is the time to apply what you have learned. What I would like for you to do is find some powerful men in your community, job, church, family, and city that have rose to the occasion and defeated any negative opinion, circumstance, or situation that was placed before them. Connect with these men on a deeper level. Make phone calls, home visitation, or invite them out for lunch and find out what motivates them to keep moving forward. Be open-minded and have an open heart to the knowledge, wisdom, and leadership skills that will be offered unto you. Overall, let them know you care, and you are serious about making improvements to your life. The purpose of this assignment is for you to see firsthand that there are men around that may have been in similar positions that you are in or facing similar problems and this will keep you moving past the negativity. Stay connected with these men because anything you may face; you will have them in your corner to provide you with knowledge and wisdom to get beyond it and prosper.

CHAPTER THREE

Just Stand Tall

Imagine riding around your city during a rainy day. On this ride, you see trash cans being blown over, debris bellowing all over the road, trees blowing in the wind, and some guy walking in the rain. You pass by many office buildings and realize that these buildings have not been impacted by the dangerous winds and rains. The windows are intact, the doors are nicely on the hinges: the building is simply standing strong ready for business as if this perilous weather is not happening. You begin to wonder why the buildings are able to endure weather and any type of conditions. The answer is quite simple--these buildings have a solid foundation that was set-up to withstand any weathering conditions. With that being said, when it rains, sleets, or snows, these buildings are able to stand tall by design. My brotha, you must be just like these buildings and stand tall when you are experiencing troublesome weathers and powerful storms in your life. It all starts with a blueprint for surviving disasters and building the strong, firm foundation that will last.

When you were created, you were given a mind, a body, and a spirit that you must continuously develop and strengthen as the days go by. Each has an importance in being able to have endurance, strength, and wisdom to stand tall during life's weakest, lowest, darkest moments. My brotha: if you spend time working on these areas, you will continue to see and feel an increase in your elevation. Do you think the engineers who designed those buildings from earlier stopped when they laid the first bricks and boards down? Of course, you know the answer is no. The engineers spent time working on the foundation and improving their progress until the building was finished and the foundation was solid as a rock. As a man, you should have the same concepts and mentality when it comes to your foundation. You should work to strengthen your mind, body, and spirit so that, when you experience a heavy rainfall or strong snowstorm in your life, you will not be easily moved. When the winds get heavy, you will not be as shaky as a small tree in your neighbor's newly landscaped front lawn. As a result, you will be able to shake off the dirt, dust, and debris; stand tall; and resume reaching for your goals in life.

Renovations are always an effective act as well. After a massive storm such as Hurricane Katrina, many homes and buildings were destroyed or highly damaged to the foundation, requiring some intense renovations. As you may know, renovations are not quick and simple: they require a plethora of thought, strategic planning, and proficient financing. The damaged components must be removed, and the area should be free of debris before the rebuilding can take place. The objectives of the renovations are not only to strengthen the foundation even more but also to provide the building with a new, innovative look. My brotha, would it be safe to say that you can perform some renovations in your life? Let's begin to see how this life-changing task can be done.

The first action you want to do is identify the damaged components in your life that require attention. This is an important step because you don't want any repairs to go unnoticed as you move to reconstruct your life. Carefully examine yourself and evaluate where you want to get stronger and better. Once this is done, you should create a nice, well- thought-out, "how-to" plan. By "how-to," I'm asking, how you are going to successfully correct these problems and make these renovations? For myself, when my daughter was born, I knew I needed to make some renovations in my own life. I knew in order to be an effective father, I needed to make some necessary changes to my foundation. First thing I did was defined my very own definition of what it meant to be a father. Secondly, I identified the action steps I needed to take to meet my own definition. Thirdly, I made a commitment to be the best father to the highest capacity. I started my "how-to" plan with the end in mind. I was forward thinking and visualized how I wanted to be as a father and spent time becoming him. Your plan will require some deep self-assessing and personal convictions. Remember, this should not be a simple and quick process; therefore, really spend the necessary time to come up with some strategic, effective ways to build a better *you*! As you complete your how-to plan, the final step to do is begin the renovation process. Your goal throughout this process is to be a more powerful, innovative, recreated version of yourself. When all of the reconstruction is complete, you will be able to handle any circumstance that comes your way. Just like the buildings mentioned earlier, people will see you and wonder how you're able to conquer all of the storms you've been through. Now that your mind, body, and spirit are stronger than before, you're able to stand tall and grow forevermore.

Principles

Standing tall after being knocked down is one of the hardest actions to accomplish. Your pride is hurt, your self-esteem is lowered, and your attitude regarding life suffers greatly. You think to yourself, "how can I go on?" or "how can I get back up after this?" The truth of the matter is, my brotha, you must get back up, even when the pain and misery is unbearable. It's a test of strength, a test of faith, and a test to your overall well-being as a man. In the words of the powerful motivational speaker Les Brown, "If you fall, fall on your back. If you can look up, you can get it".

Source: What to do when you fee lost by Les Brown

Here are a few principles to live through the oppression being a better you:

A. Pain is only temporary. You may be hurting now, but all pain results in healing. It's like a bruise. The body's natural response is to be alarmed with pain, but, once the pain subsides, the body begins the healing process.

B. Bigger and better. When you get knocked down, you can spring back into a bigger and better position in life. Think about the process when you upgrade your cellular phone. When your old phone begins to fail, you look to upgrade it to a bigger and better device.

C. It's your mentality that counts. Thoughts become actions, so if you can think it then you can do it. Your progress slowly depends on your mindset.

Adhere to these words and you will soon realize that standing tall after falling is a game-changing event for your life.

Applying the Lesson

At some point in life, we all have had some form of disappointment that has knocked us down and off course from the path we were set on. These mishaps are not cruelties we would wish on our worst enemy yet going through them has made us wiser as men. At this time, I would like for you to just reflect on all the disappointments you've encountered in your life. Write these experiences down on index cards, post-it notes, or some form of small sheet of paper. As you finish, compile all the paper, place it in a bag, take it to the backyard, and set it on fire or place the paper in the fireplace. These experiences do not define you nor did they break you. Because of these experiences, your foundation is much stronger than ever before.

CHAPTER FOUR

Trust Yourself

There's a saying that asserts, "Life is what you make of it, so take control and make the best of it." When you are in complete control of your life, the opportunities are endless, but you must give yourself a try and tap into your true potential to manifest your destiny. Imagine a society where Dr. Martin Luther King Jr. didn't realize his true potential. Imagine how life would be if Dr. King did not take charge in his efforts to lead people to the "Promised Land." Dr. King had a divine calling for his life, spent his life fulfilling that calling, and was assassinated because of fighting for a dream that he believed in. Of course, he had his own internal battles, but his focus was fixed on the future for others--not just himself. Dr. King did not allow all the negative circumstances of the world to deter him from his path and neither should you.

Dr. King knew there were multitudes of generations counting on him to believe in himself and to believe that God will guide him through the difficult process. If Dr. King could manifest his destiny, live out his purpose, and make a historical impact as his legacy lives on today, then what is it that is stopping you? My brotha, this may not be an easy question to answer, but it must be addressed. Ask yourself, "Is it fear-related?" You are not alone. Every great influencer of this world and every successful being to grace the Earth had to deal with some form of fear. The key is to focus your attention on facing that fear and overcoming it. Dale Carnegie, a famous writer on self-improvement and interpersonal skills, once said, "If you want to conquer fear, don't sit at home and think about it. Go out and get busy." You must get out of your own way and conquer the fear because, if you don't, then you will never know how great you truly can be.

Defeating fear truly means to try and trust yourself because you are more than a conqueror and have the power to advance past any test that stands in your way. Winning this battle does not require any special mechanical tools or magical resources: it simply means you are acknowledging your ability to dismantle your fears just as those before you have been able to do. Once you understand your power, you will realize the fears you have are not superior and you will be able to progress in your journey to your potential. The sooner you apply pressure to your true being, the greater your life will evolve. Now that the fear has been addressed, consider what else could be holding you back from stepping forward.

Procrastination also has a negative impact on purpose progression. At this very moment, think of how long you have had the desire to start your own business. Think about the amount of time you have spent drafting the ideas for your nonprofit organization. How long has it been since you started drafting that unfinished writing project you've been talking about? There has been plenty of time for you to complete your goals, but you have allowed fear to control you and procrastination to prevent you from progressing towards your true potential.

Les Brown once stated, "Too many of us are not living our dreams because we are living our fears!" Let this statement resonate in your mind for just a moment. Here it is again: "Too many of us are not living our dreams because we are living our fears!" Some people are so far consumed with fear that life passes them by, and they are no further on their course than where they started. In the words of the great, legendary rapper Lil Wayne, "Fear is a weak emotion." It is safe to state that weak-minded individuals live in fear! The weak-minded allow fear to control their lives and dictate what to think, how to feel, and what to do. The weak-minded are comfortable living in fear because it is the normal standard in their lives.

Source: You have the power to change by Les Brown

For you, it does not have to be the same! "Ultimately, we deeply know on the other side of fear is freedom," said Marilyn Ferguson. If you can get past your fears, you can break down the barriers blocking you from your freedom. Develop the courage and faith in yourself. Understand that God did not give us the spirit of fear--he granted us the power to outlive any obstacle and progress past any problem. Your potential to succeed depends on your ability to shake down those fear-barring shackles and try yourself. You've let fear win this battle for far too long and it is time to win the war. It is your moment to reach down inside of yourself and grab hold of the person you are truly meant to be in this life. Try yourself! Place a bet on yourself and find a way to succeed in your efforts. Test your true abilities and I guarantee the future version of who you are will be grateful for you stepping up to the challenge, defeating your fears, and winning the wars in your life. You can do zero harm by taking a chance on yourself and seeing what you are truly capable of accomplishing when you put your mind and heart into everything you aspire to do. Your victories, your successes, and your legacy all fall on your decision to no longer deny yourself the freedom you deserve.

Choosing your freedom is an ongoing decision because life has a way of throwing fear-based obstacles across your path. You may have experienced plenty of these obstacles before, but, when you are on the path to freedom, the forces are intensified. Through being tough and tight, you must still choose freedom. Kevyn Aucoin, a phenomenal American makeup artist, photographer, and author, presents the key to freedom in this eloquently spoken declaration:

Love myself I do. Not everything, but I love good as well as the bad. I love my crazy lifestyle, and I love my hard discipline. I love my freedom of speech and the way my eyes get dark when I'm tired. I love that I have learned to trust people with my heart, even if it will get broken. I am proud of everything I am and will become.

Not only does trusting yourself allow you to be free, it also allows you to love everything about you, your life, and everyone around you. This is the type of freedom that makes life worthwhile. This is the type of freedom you receive when you develop the trust within yourself in making the conscious decision that fear no longer exists in your life. From this moment forward, make the declaration that your trust in yourself will outlive any fear or doubt.

Principles – T.R.U.S.T.

Developing trust is never an easy concept; however, it is an essential skill that must be mastered over time. In her popular book, *Trust,* Iyanla Vanzant stated:

Trust is a function of choice. Trust grows in hearts that have often been broken open by pain. Trust can unfold in response to devastation, disappointment, and, more often than not, a depth of dysfunction that threatens the human soul.

Source: Trust by Iyanla Vanzant

Here you see the significance of fine-tuning your ability to trust. It is not an emotion: trust is a verb that comes to life in action. You must care for your ability to trust as it is another one of life's most precious jewels. If you cannot trust yourself, then you will not be able to love yourself and if you cannot love yourself, you will not be able to love others nor allow yourself to be loved. To fully understand the trust concept, let's break it down and spell it out: T.R.U.S.T.

T is for time. There is no limit to the amount of time it will take to master trust. The time is solely dependent upon your actions and desire to trust. Put forth the effort and learn about yourself and you will be able to trust yourself in allotted time.

R is for reassurance. You can be reassured that developing the ability to trust is a valuable life skill. It will benefit your life greatly as you will be able sustain healthy relationships. Trust will enable you to experience freedom and pure happiness.

U is for understanding. Through mastering truth, you understand what it means to trust. It is your understanding that grants you the wisdom and authority to develop and possess trust during everything you experience.

S is for sacrifice. Trust is a game of sacrifices. When learning to trust, you must sacrifice your old, non-trustworthy habits because you are pursuing a new, bright beginning.

T is for transformation. You will experience an extraordinary shift in your life when you develop the ability to trust. Your life and perception will transform in ways you could not imagine.

Don't waste any more time, unable to trust yourself and trust others who are in your life. Keep your heart and mind fixed on pursuing your freedom and the future you have always wanted. It is time for your light to shine in a new direction.

Applying the Lesson

Over the course of your life, you have endured some experiences and life-changing circumstances that have altered your trust. These experiences have haunted you for far too long and have hindered you from progressing in life. Now is the time to let those obstacles decease out of your memory! Here is a best practice that will allow you to release all those demons out of your spirit. For the next 21 days, you are to write out every negative circumstance, or ones that you can recall, and cast them out of your spiritual treasure chest. Then, burn your list, bury it, or simply toss it in the trash: but the objective is to release that energy out of your life. Document your feelings afterwards and continue to this practice until you have become fearless and have overcome your inability to trust.

CHAPTER FIVE

New Opportunities

Every man deserves a second chance at life when he's had a troublesome past. It is not uncommon for a man to spend his youthful years engaged in meaningless activities and must deal with the consequences as he grows older. Take a moment and think about the men behind the prison bars; at one point in time, they were once free men living a life full of opportunities but became mixed up in the wrong activities. Some of these men will spend the remainder of their life behind bars while others have the possibility to walk out the prison doors back into civilization. The men who regain their freedom can look towards the future and capitalize on the new opportunities to right their wrongs and build a sustainable, productive life.

Men who have served their time, paid their dues, and cleared their names should not have to suffer for events performed in the past. Society has a way of making these men feel worse about themselves because of what happened rather than to help them pursue the valuable benefits that could potentially be in their paths. To my brothas who are experiencing such circumstances: you must understand that you are not your past. Know that you are not alone because there are plenty of men who faced similar defeating objectives but came out on the winning side of it all. The key to winning amongst these circumstances is to capitalize on the new opportunities to advance and stabilize your life.

Opportunities will come your way, but you must be in the retrieving position and maneuver in the right direction. When you are presented with an opportunity to start on a new path, do not take it for granted. Take any opportunity and make the absolute best of it because life has zero guarantees. You are not guaranteed to obtain another opportunity. You are not guaranteed another chance to recreate your life in a new light and positive direction;

therefore, when it comes, grab a hold to the opportunity and give it everything that you have inside of you!

Opportunities should be followed by gratitude and appreciation. Every man that has a rough background does not receive the same opportunities to start over. Every man does not have the liberty to pick up where he left off before he made those terrible discussions. So, it is important for you to acknowledge your privilege and appreciate your opportunities whether expected or unexpected. Each new opportunity will have a specific purpose for your life, and it is your responsibility to determine the lesson and the knowledge that you must gain from it all. This is the point of your life that you have been praying for and patiently waiting on the golden opportunity to make your name be mentioned in a positive arena.

With new opportunities and second chances, there should be humbleness. My brothas, remember to remain humble throughout your life journey of redirection and refocus. I encourage to do some rededication to your core values and principles as these will be your accountability tools to prevent you from going down the wrong path and making the same devastating mistakes. Again, this is your opportunity to create a new mentality and develop a new outlook on life because you have a chance to rebuild and revitalize everything, which could have been lifeless.

Optimism is the fuel required to keep you on your path and on your feet in this new day. Optimism can be defined as the hopefulness and confidence about the future or the successful outcome of something. When it comes to new opportunities, you may experience some doubt in your ability to make the right decisions and this is perfectly normal behavior. You will experience some nervousness and anxiety when embraced by second chances and opportunities to do things differently.

Do not be alarmed nor dismayed if life becomes a little rough and rocky on voyage to brighter days. If you keep moving forward, one step at a time, the ride will get a little smoother and the resistance will become a little easier. Your feelings will subside and your eagerness will begin to grow because you are moving into a new direction, a decision that may have seemed impossible when you were living on the inside behind those metal and mental bars. It is time to shake off the negative energy and put on a new crown of positive outlook because new opportunities, new journeys, and new memories are coming your way.

Principles – G.R.O.W.T.H.

To make the most out of new opportunities, it is going to require a new outlook and positive behavior. Negativity is a blocker of anything promising and prosperous that will come into your life. The key to overcoming negativity is to live in optimism. To live in the land of opportunity, it starts with your perception of everything happens over the course of your life. Bob Feller, describe credibility, once asserted that: "Every day is a new opportunity. You can build on yesterday's success or put its failures behind and start over again. That's the way life is…" See everything in the optimistic viewpoint. Make it your mission to always see the opportunity when it is most difficult to remain positive.

G is for giving up all the negativity and letting go of your former self. You must give up the bad to receive the good.

R is for the righteous response to being provided with the chance to correct your previous mistakes. Second chances are rewards because for some, they are not rendered the same.

O is for the optimistic personality required to capitalize on the various opportunities over the horizon. If you can see the good, everything will be good.

W is for the continuous work to obtain the wonders of this lifetime. Workout physically, mentally, and spiritually so that you can be the best version of yourself.

T is for teachable. Your past should serve as teachable moments. You do not want to make the same mistakes twice and void all your ongoing progress.

H is for habit. Develop some positive elevating habits that give you overwhelming positive energy.

Applying the Lesson

There are zero benefits with knowledge if you are not applying the information to your life. I am certain you have been approached by some opportunities to do something differently but, as aforementioned, you may have been living in self-doubt and uncertainty. To truly manage and maximize your opportunities, you need to develop an optimizing plan. What we are going to do is set you up on a 21-day optimization plan and it will be extremely simple. For the next 21 days, you are to identify each maximizing opportunity that you encounter each day. For example, today you may have the opportunity to exercise with a fitness group or you may be invited to learn a new skill. The key concept is for you to embed your mind with positivity and creativity to create a new, rewarding path for yourself. Opportunities are all around you, but it is your responsibility to be present and available to cease them. At the end of the 21 days, you're going view life with a different eyesight.

CHAPTER SIX

Changing Directions

The ultimate measure of life is growth and growth occur in many different areas of life and comes in many forms. When you set goals for your life, essentially, you have a pre-established plan of everything you aspire to accomplish. Your plan is uniquely crafted to match your desires and attributions. Within your plan, you have specific timeframes attached to goals because you believe your plan is set and nothing will come about to deter you from life objectives. Ultimately, we all want a flawless journey to success, but circumstances may occur to modify your pace to your finish line. Much like a GPS, when you make a wrong turn on your route, my brotha, you will be instructed to change directions so you can reach your destination.

The first area you experience some rerouting may be or has been in education. Most people determine in high school the ideal profession they wish to pursue. The majority have the goal set to attend a college or university because of the stories from others, freedom, or the social attraction portrayed on movies and television shows. The truth is, not everyone has the luxury or financial support to attend a four-year institution, meaning they must reroute to other options. There are also people who may have faced some difficulty in high school and had to pursue alternative routes to a high school diploma. The fact remains that, as the old folks like to say, "There is more than one way to skin a cat," so don't be alarmed if you must go in a different direction.

The next rerouting must deal with faith-based practices or religion. From childhood to early stages of adulthood, many people grew up practicing some form of religion because it was a part of their family culture. Sundays meant going to the church for hours, and as a child, you either participated in the choir or you were a junior usher. While living under your parents' roof, you did not have the option nor freedom to decide how you wanted to enhance your spiritual development. As an adult, you can now enjoy the freedom of spiritual growth. If you grew up Baptist, you can convert to another practice. You can change direction in your spiritual walk, if you stay on the right path. The more you research, the more you will learn there is more than one way to accomplish the righteous goal and reach the divine destination.

Changing directions often happens in the areas of employment. People will pursue a job opportunity and spend years in this position only to realize that is it not the ideal career for them. Staying in a job unfitting to your desires could potentially lead to a life of stress and deep depression. Barely making ends meet and having nothing to show for your hard work leaves an individual frustrated with the idea of the "American Dream." Society tells you to go to college, work 40-50 years of your life, only to retire on an extremely small fraction of your worth. This is the "American Dream" they have painted so glamorously over the decades yet in today's society, the "American Dream" sounds much like a nightmare on Elm Street. It is scary to know you must spend nearly 75% of your life working jobs, while suffering mentally, emotionally, and spiritually, to build a life that you were taught to pursue. For those who want to walk a different path, I encourage to do exactly that; be different. Rerouting your career to a new profession is not an easy task but it is very rewarding; also, it is the right thing to do when your mental health begins to decline. There are many different professions in the job market and entrepreneurship is an available decision that has sparked growth in present-day society. If you have reached a dead-end in your present employment, now is the time for you to pull out your goal map and seek a novel, refreshing route that gives you fulfillment.

It is important to mention that, just as leaving unfulfilling employment, you have the right to cut ties with a negative, draining environment. If the community you are residing in does not offer economic development, sufficient education, and recreational activities for family fun, you have the right to leave. Being in a compulsive community may deter your progress when you striving to transform into a new being. You do not have to settle for this mediocrity, and you are not required to stay in these devastating circumstances. Examine your life objectives, study different prosperous areas, and develop a strategic plan to transition you from the dark place to a bright, greater place for your livelihood. There are times when a new scenery is the answer to all problems you may be experiencing. A new living domicile and a new community could present you with a better outlook on life. Your vision is clearer, and your energy is revitalized because you no longer have to endure the restrictions or limitations. Rid yourself of the extreme exhaustion and elevate as you accelerate towards your destiny because you decided to change directions.

Changing directions is one of the best things you could do with your life. No one deserves to be stuck in a situation regardless if life throws a wicked curveball or not. There are always other options available, even if you have not been made aware. Muscle up the courage and declare to yourself that your life is more valuable than what you are currently experiencing. Despite what people say, you must act in the manner that is beneficial and brings you closer to the life of your dreams. With determination, dedication, and self-discovery, changing directions will lead you to the best days for the rest of your life.

Principles – C.H.A.N.G.E.

One of the greatest joys of life is knowing that, as people, we have the ability to make a change to any issue that is less desirable or anything not in our best interest. The key is to identify what is not making us happy and to be intentional about creating change in our lives.

C is for the corrections and creativity you must develop once you decide change is needed in your life. Corrections don't mean anything is wrong: it just means old ways are no longer effective and creativity is needed to implement new methods.

H stands for the happiness you are seeking in a new direction. Happiness is internal and you must define everything that makes you happy.

A is for the adventures that will emerge from this brave, new journey. Of course, the journey is scary, but it will also be fun as you discover a new you.

N happens to stand for new and now. The longer you wait, the longer you will take to live in and receive the abundance of your decision to seek a new scenery.

G is for guidance because this journey of change will require some guidance. Make some valuable connections who will not steer you in the wrong direction.

E stands for elevation and embrace. This brave new journey should bring excitement and be embraced with high energy.

Remember, nothing changes unless your attitude, behavior, mentality, and actions change. In order to fully change directions in your life, you must embrace the principles of change and adhere to them for the remainder of your days.

Applying the Lesson

My brotha, you are not the only person that has decided to seek a new life in a different direction. There are men who have been succeeding on different paths because they decided that a brand-new life would bring them more happiness and fulfillment than their previous lifestyle. You must understand you do not have to take this journey alone and it will be beneficial for you to seek supportive counsel. As you begin to reroute your life, conduct some research and reach out to the guys who will be of guidance to you. Make a refined list of everything you wish to be different and start with one direction at a time. Start with the easiest thing to change to the most difficult and approach every area with determination. My brotha, when you execute this list, your life will start to change like clockwork.

CHAPTER SEVEN

Milestones

There is an old saying that states maturity does not come with age--it comes by the way of time and experience. These experiences, rather good or bad, are to be considered milestones that aids in mental strength and development. The online dictionary defines milestones as the actions or events marking a significant change or stage in development. Based off the definition, every one of us have reached some major milestones in our lifetime. Some may be faint in memory and others are as clear as day but all of them have made us into the people we are today.

Milestones should be celebrated, appreciated, and advanced when you obtain new experiences and develop new knowledge. From newborns to toddlers and teenagers to adults, we have experienced events that have allowed us to mature in our thoughts, actions, and emotions. Because of these moments, we can live with a multitude of memories to serve as guides and outlines for the next steps in life. Some have more milestones than others and it is important to note that every milestone is going to be personal to each individual.

There should be milestones you want to meet in every aspect of your life. As men, we have multiple roles, and, just like our goals, we should want to be successful and accomplish every milestone set in our paths. But, in order to do so, we must first recall the milestones already attained and establish new milestones to meet. You can't forecast where you want to go until you acknowledge where you have been. If you have ever played sports, think of milestones as the highlights of your career and how you could improve your game.

Milestones are the remarkable experiences resulting in many intangible rewards. As an infant, some accomplished milestones were developing teeth, learning how to crawl, cognitive development, and motor intuition. Of course, these advances did not happen overnight; it took time. From toddler days to being a little kid, you gained mobility to freely move around and complete actions on your own, such as feeding, bathing, walking/running, and climbing. You reached a milestone in achieving a small sense of independence. As a teenager to adulthood, your milestones increase because there are grand amounts of experiences over the horizon for you.

Milestones are measurements of growth and advancement. Imagine being in a science lab conducting an experiment and you wanted to check your data according to the guidelines. If your experiment does not align with the guidelines, then you must do a little more work for everything to be enough. Now, with milestones, there is not a guaranteed timeline of events because moments happen in life that alter experiences. You can experiment with a variety of tools, but it will only be successful based on the milestone you are striving to achieve.

Do not take any of your experiences for granted because everything has a significant meaning that may be indescribable at the moment. There is nothing that happens by coincidence. Every moment of your life and every milestone you have succeeded is more valuable than what is on the outer surface. To fully understand what your milestones truly mean, you must mute all outside noise and stay connected with the higher power. No--that does not mean put yourself in an asylum of isolation, but it is rewarding to spend time alone in pursuit of your self-discovery. Remember, authentic elevation does require some form of separation and when you're in separation, you are in preparation for more.

Succeeding with your milestones takes time; however, it should not take too much of your time. In order to reach every milestone, it is highly advised to secure an accountability partner or power circle to keep you on track. Their purpose is not to give you orders nor do the work for you but to ensure you are doing work on yourself. You cannot and will not reach your milestones unless you view them as actual achievements like the vision to manifest, purpose to fulfill, and the goals you have set to accomplish. Don't waste any more time on actions that lack importance because the next level of your life depends greatly on what you are doing now.

Principles – M.I.L.E.S.T.O.N.E.S.

Milestones are substantial assets to your life and should be unlimited and based off the positions you wish to fulfill with your life. They are not chores nor obligations but more like life and career objectives.

Manpower will give you the strength and courage to push past any circumstances. Make sure you stay activated on your journey.

Information provides resources on how to accomplish a task that you may find difficult. Seek information when necessary.

Listen to solid advice from your power circle. They want to see you advance and succeed.

Exercise to keep your body operational. You cannot be productive with an unhealthy, sluggish mentality.

Solidify your presence where you are now. There is strength to gain on every stage of the process.

Time is of the essence. As noted, take your time but do not take too much time and miss out on meaningful opportunities because you were not ready.

Opinions of your milestones are totally irrelevant. This is your life and only you know where you want to go and what you want to obtain.

Never take an experience for granted. It may have a deeper understanding that requires some in depth meditation.

Exemplify what it means to be devoted to the grind. Get to work even when you do not feel like completing any task.

Save the excuses for someone who cares.

Applying the Lesson

As mentioned in the chapter, in order to understand where you want to go, you must first acknowledge where you have been. Now is the time to make a mark of your milestones. You can use index cards, a notebook, a legal pad, or poster board, but the objective for you is to draft all your successful milestones and place a check next to each item. After you place a check, write out the experience and what it has taught you and apply every lesson to the next milestones to achieve. If you have visuals, use them to increase the excitement of succeeding and electrify your drive to get to the next milestone. Accountability is a must so connect with your power circle once a month to track your progress.

CHAPTER EIGHT

Success Story

Everybody has their own version of a success story that originated from a season of struggles. There are people who have spent decades in the trenches before they obtained success and gained sunshine after years of nonstop rainy days. Look at the stories of men like Steve Harvey, Tyler Perry, or Kevin Hart and understand that success is attainable to anyone who is willing to work hard. These three gentlemen, amongst others, of course, decided to work hard with their gifts and passions. They knew there was a success story with their names on it and it was their responsibility to ensure that all their goals and dreams became true. My brothas, you must determine the depth of your success story.

Any success is better than none at all and it is defined by your work ethic. Writing your success story will require some blood, sweat, and tears: what the greats call sweat equity. You cannot be afraid to get your hands dirty or experience war wounds from the bumps and bruises that come throughout this process. If you are a fan of football, then you would see players like NFL star, Benjamin Watson of the Baltimore Ravens, know a lot about having a dedicated work ethic when he contemplates: "God blessed me with great talent and good genetics. Plus, he blessed me with a good work ethic and a drive to want the best." If you examine the context of this statement, you will understand that having great talent is only half the battle. You must back up your talent with a meticulous work ethic to capture your level of greatness.

When crafting your success story, understand there will be people rooting against you disguised as supporters. They will walk with you, talk with you, and then leave you to talk negatively about you behind your back. There will be people preying against you and wanting to see you defeated, discouraged, and devastated. To truly advance past these wolves, you must stay disciplined and devoted to your cause. Your focus should always be on future and securing your success story. Do not give people the power over your potential. Overcome their judgements because opinions of negative people have zero benefits in being successful.

Make your success story highlight the successes in your life, not others. When you are on this path to personal greatness, it is important not to attempt to ride the coattails of other people's successes. Yes, you can seek advisement from people who are doing what you aspire to do, but the difference is your success is yours and yours only. Your mentors cannot and will not do the work for you and you cannot expect their wealth and riches to become yours because you are aspiring to be in the same industry. You must take the blueprint given and redefine the steps to meet your anticipated outcome.

From sweat equity to branding your own success, you must understand that your season will come if you stay in the process. Seriously, you must stay committed to making your success a true reality. It cannot happen if you leave the process before you and begin to see everything come into fruition. Imagine you spend five to ten years in constant grind and you throw in the towel right before the biggest break of your life. Seriously take a moment and think about that for a second. Dedicating five to ten years and giving up when your reward was around the corner will leave you devastated and defeated. So, stay in the battle, keep fighting, but do not quit because the process works as long as you have trust in yourself and believe in your ability to be successful.

You do not need any magical spells, secret ingredients, or top of the line equipment to create your successful story. What you need is already embedded inside of you and you must possess the will to bring it out of you. At the end of the day, your story is not going to write itself and you cannot expect moments to just automatically happen without you exerting any energy. Your energy, your efforts, and your enormous focus are required for everything to be composed and completed in your success story. When you are doing everything expected of you, blocks will begin to fall into place and flow in the right direction. The real magic is in your mindset and maintaining your momentum through the finish line. Success is yours so keep writing every chapter of your story.

Principles – S.T.O.R.Y.

Success does not come easy for anyone unless they have royal blood, or you have inherited the family's fortune and businesses. Otherwise, success requires hard work, dedication, tough skin, and daily devotion. It also demands acknowledgement of the pen being in your hand to do the writing of this story of your accomplishments.

Survival of the good days and bad days of productivity. Some days you will be sluggish, but you must push through and make every day count.

Trace over the blueprints of others but make alterations to match your values and ideals of success. Every objective should be appropriately crafted to your uniqueness.

Occasional breaks are important to your success. To prevent burnout, ensure you implement breaks to refresh, refine, and revitalize all your energy and focus.

Reconstruction of your life is ideal if you have not been experiencing much success. If you have been in the slumps without any happiness, it is time to reconstruct and refocus your attention on the prize that is ahead.

Yield to anything that promotes a danger to your story or anything that could potentially harm you in anyway; take precautions.

Again, you are the answer and it is your responsibility to take ownership of your story. You are in control of the way it is written; no one else but you.

Applying the Lesson

Knowing what you want out of life is critical and necessary to work towards your success story. If you do not know what you want, you cannot be in pursuit of it and you are merely just freestyling your way through life. Therefore, if you are lost and confused about the direction of your life, then it is highly recommended for you to take some "me time" and meditate on your future. After your meditation, grab a pen and pad and begin to write what you want your life to look like in the next decade. Really think about the life you want and be specific as you write out this proclamation. Once you have completed your ideal life with all the specifics, you must place this documentation all over your house and declare that you will spend the remainder of your days writing your success story and bringing your ideal life into complete manifestation.

CHAPTER NINE

Give Back

When you reach the pinnacle of success, never forget where you started, how you started, and everything you had to endure to reach the top. Know that you have been blessed to be in the position to spread the wealth and knowledge, so you can empower the next generation of success stories. Ask yourself what good is it to reach a leadership position and not reach back to develop more leaders to follow in your footsteps? The way to stay success is to continuously empower and develop other people into leaders in their respective industries. When you give back with your life, you will gain more than you can acquire through service.

You should be the type of leader, mentor, and role model you needed when you were in the trenches. A leader is an individual who knows what it takes to succeed. A leader leads with action and shows people that it is possible to succeed and win. A mentor is a person that offers advice and guidance to the hungry, ambitious believers. A mentor empowers people to take charge and pursue their goals. A role model is not always a professional athlete, rapper, or entertainer. A role model can be someone who shares similarities with the underprivileged, makes it to the top by defeating the adversity, and defies the odds. The starlight nor popularity are a requirement for you to be considered either. The only requirement is a humble spirit, helping heart, and a giving mentality.

You can give back to others with your gifts and passions. If you are a gifted teacher or educator, seek opportunities to give back where you can serve by teaching. You can offer boot-camps if you are gifted in exercise science and fitness training. Maybe you are highly skilled in photography and videography: you could take your talents to the schools and offer to take class pictures and video school dances for keepsakes. Whatever your gifts may be, it would be completely selfish of you to refrain from sharing them when that is the purpose for you having those gifts. Bring your gifts to your home communities and any place where you think they are beneficial. When you are in the position to give back, do just that! Keep in mind, people seeing you operating in your gifts will propel them to engage and act to discover, develop, and discipline themselves to function in their gifted areas. With your gifts, you could be the gift and solution to everyone you are connected to and the people you come across.

Be enthused and intentional when opportunities to give come across your path. Giving back to the less fortunate and disadvantaged should be a noble deed of honor. Do not give back for the recognition or praise because that means your heart is not in the right place and you are seeking self-gratification. Give back because you are helping people who may lack the opportunities elsewhere. Do good because you know service is the way to true impact and influence amongst the generations. The brilliant theoretical physicist, Albert Einstein, once stated, "Only a life lived for others is a life worthwhile," meaning we should life to serve others. Imagine the lives you could touch when you become a giver. The thought of reaching lives should create an everlasting fire inside of you that cannot burn out because it is one of life's purposeful missions.

When you have sustained your success and outreach opportunities, you will be known as a philanthropist because at the heart and soul of giving back is to promote human welfare. Most of the successful leaders are philanthropists because they understand constantly acting with their giving endeavors is the way to true influence and to increase the support of their followers. The more you give, the more you can grow and develop in your mission. Acknowledge there is always another level of success to reach once you make it to the big leagues so why not make it a goal to master the art of giving back? At the end of day, more joy comes from blessing others. Just examine all the people you follow, and you will understand that giving back provides you with fulfillment at any level of success. You are blessed to be a blessing, so do not take your position, your power, or your potential to grow others for granted. You made it, therefore, reach back and help others do the same.

We learn that sharing is caring at an early stage of life. Of course, initially we did not want to share because we wanted everything to ourselves. We wanted to gain but we did not like the idea of giving anything away. As maturity increases and experiences broaden, you will know that giving back to others will show people the compassion that you possess. Everything that you will do is of good work and it all will be a part of your legacy. Don't be like your younger self and only seek to gain from the world. Change your perspective and search for the chance to give the world what you have gained. And when you come from a good place, your efforts will be priceless.

Principles – G.I.V.I.N.G.

Giving back to others should be at the top of the list for every individual that is winning on any level of success. The reality is some people are immoral and lack to the compassion to help others. Giving back may not solve all the problems people face, but it will soothe their wounds as they continue to seek meaningful solutions. You are not the healer, but you can always offer resourceful ways to help people.

Generosity is the word you want people to describe you as. Behave, maneuver, and exert a great array of energy where people want to connect with you. Give more of yourself to others.

Influence other people with your giving. The more you give back, the more influence you will have amongst people.

Victory is yours and you can share it with other people. Don't turn your back on the individuals who helped you reach your full potential. A win for you is a win for them as well.

Impress upon people the power to overcome and excel through your contributions. Giving with a purpose will leave an everlasting impression.

Neglect your old ways of thinking when it comes to giving back to others. Sharing with others is the way you show people how much you care.

Grant people the opportunity to hear your story of success. Your story is more valuable than you think.

Take these principles and embed them in your mind. When you are approached by a community service agent with an upcoming project, the decision to participate will come easy. In a small sense, all of us have been on the receiving end of someone else's contributions so keep that in mind as you move forward.

Applying the Lesson

Your life has been compiled of a substantial amount of different experiences that has afforded you valuable wisdom and knowledge. Whether you are at the top of your life or you are striving to reach the top, someone somewhere has given you something that helped you throughout your journey. Your next assignment is to ponder on your childhood, teenage years, and/or adult life thus far. Think about every person who has given you something that has been beneficial to your life. Rather it be small, big, or enormous--if it was given to you and played a major role in your success, it counts. Now, with all these thoughts in mind, you are to write a letter explaining everything which was given to you and express your gratitude for it all. If you feel compelled to mail out the letter, that is fine, but the objective is to get you to understand the value of giving back to others as a testament of your own life. Again, as previously stated, leaders understand that importance of giving back to others.

CHAPTER TEN

Live Abundantly

Many people go through life in survival mode and hardly experience the true joys of having success. And because they are living in survival mode, goals go unnoticed, dreams begin to fade, and life gets harder as the days pass. That old "American Dream" that everyone strives to fulfill really begins to look like an old urban legend written by some chaotic person. The fight to live abundantly seems like a beautiful dream on paper, but truth being told, it is a scary nightmare that may cost you sleep at night. However, when you work hard and continue to invest in yourself, you will see the fruit of your labor and the idea of living abundantly becomes a little more realistic.

Living abundantly or living life in full, simply means acquiring more and doing more than you were to do before. It means you are committed to your goals, in sync with your vision, and you know your dreams are within your reach. American author, Marianne Williamson, comments that "The key to abundance is meeting limited circumstances with unlimited thoughts." You must move past mediocrity, cancel out any chaos, and endure any painful emotions during the process.

You must learn to control the circumstances and not allow the circumstances to control you. Far too often people allow their circumstances to dictate their life without seeing these moments in a different perspective. Losing a job is not the end of the world. Experiencing car malfunctions is not the end of the world. Being homeless or living out of hotels, by any means, is not the end of the world. It is the way your mind processes these events that holds the key to control. When you have a shifting mindset, losing a job means there is a greater position coming your way. With a newly shifted mindset, mechanical issues could present a sign for you to get a new car. A person with a renewed mind could view homelessness as a wisdom experience and become highly motivated to become a homeowner. All of this may sound bizarre, but the truth is, when you have mind control over your circumstances, they cannot stop you from pursuing an abundant life.

To live abundantly means to live without any regrets because you are giving your all at everything you pursue. The proverb, "Live full; die empty," is a great explanation of this concept. When your biological clock strikes zero, you should be happy with everything you have done over the span of your life. You should be content knowing you succeeded in every endeavor. It means all your ideas did not stay ideas and you can enjoy the life you have built.

The feeling of abundance will seem like a dream come true because that is exactly what it is: a dream that became true. An abundant life will be like winning your very own crafted lottery. The more diligent you are with your numbers, the greater the rewards will be in your favor. You constantly play the numbers and you win at every level of your life, even when the odds are stacked against you. Your outlook on life is on an extremely different level. You take all those seasons of losses and transform them into winning seasons, knowing that you can live in abundance.

On the contrary, people believe having an abundant life equates to mansions, having fancy cars, and being filthy rich with more money than you can maintain. While these possessions are great, an abundant life is much more than the tangible objects. It is more than the worldly possessions. An abundant life brings more value into your life and it is symbolized by the impact you place in the world. An abundant life is shown when people know you for your works and not by the things you possess.

The world around you will change through the eyes of others. When you are living an abundant life, people will flock to your existence. When you are exceeding at a high level, people will want to be associated with you because you have excelled to a high caliber. People will witness you doing more in your life and wonder how you attracted so much success. The Hollywood Walk of Fame is composed of phenomenal individuals who excelled in their industries and are living an abundant life. The Hollywood Star is not so much about a status of wealth but more about the level of influence that people create over the span of their lives. These people are well-known not only because of the abundance of opportunities they have created for themselves but also for the abundance of opportunities they have created for others. As mentioned in the previous chapter, to experience abundance in your own life, you should provide abundance for others by accomplishing more in your life and never stopping your growth.

Principles – A.B.U.N.D.A.N.C.E.

You are only granted one life to live and your desire should be to live life abundantly. You should want more out of life than normality. You should want to be known for more than average production. The conclusion of your life should not only consist of constant struggle and survival. At some point, it should turn into winning seasons and sustaining success.

Attract abundance and associate yourself with people who are doing more with their lives than the average.

Build up your confidence and speak abundance over your life and any defeating circumstances.

Utilize your connections and gifts to create the life you truly desire.

Neutralize your actions when you are dealing with emotions.

Discover what abundance means for your life and work to obtain it.

Accomplish what you can in this moment and build momentum towards your securing your future.

Natural efforts are most effective; anything forced may result in chaos.

Create your ideal life internally before you are aware of it externally.

Enjoy all the treasures and fruits of your labor as it all comes to you.

There is an abundant life for you, but it is going to require that you do more than average. You must get move past average complacency and focus on living full of happiness, peace, and success.

Applying the Lesson

An abundant life does not come by the way of wishing, hoping, and playing; it comes by the way of affirming, visualizing, praying, and acting. All that you want to accomplish, create, and develop in life is ahead of you, but you must shift into overdrive and accelerate towards the finish line. For the very last assignment of this book, you should make a list of everything that has tried to stop you, slow you down, and keep you from reaching the next level of success towards an abundant life. If you can remember any and everything from childhood to adult life, put it on paper because it is going to help you understand that none of those circumstances stopped you. On the list, identity what happened, when it happened, and how you overcame it because if you're experiencing some disruptive problems now, you have the knowledge and tools to defeat them. None of it killed you. It made you hungrier for an abundant life.

CONCLUSION

As the concluding chapter, I want to express some lasting thoughts to all my brothas, young and old, about how much I thank you for spending your time reading and applying all the lessons to your everyday life. For me, it truly means a lot to be in the position to spread words of wisdom and inspiration to every man who finds himself in his hardest moments of his life. As men, it is extremely imperative that we develop strong bonds and uplift one another because we know, "Iron sharpens Iron," as it is written in the Bible. We must set aside all our differences so that the next generation of men can have mentors and leaders and will not lack any of the knowledge, wisdom, or education needed to survive and succeed in this lifetime.

It is time for us to be the change we wish to see in the lives of all brothas. To impact someone else, every man must put forth his best effort to become the very best version of himself. Every man must change his unhealthy habits, get rid of negative thoughts, and write off anything that could be harmful to the him and every person connected to him. We must do whatever it takes to be an asset to others because being a liability is not beneficial to our growth.

It is my prayer and vision to get back to rebuilding the foundation of brotherhood and gentlemenhood that has been diminished amongst our culture of men. We have become so accustomed to building our own lives that we have forgotten about the lives of the little generation of soon-to-be men watching us. Once we reach the pinnacle of success, we forget to reach back and bolster the youth. The boys in our communities need the guidance, leadership, and the skills that we possess to become better men.

When we come together as one strong, powerful unit, there is nothing that can stop us but us. We are a strong force to be reckoned when all our strong, powerful minds stand together. There is nothing that we cannot do because we have everything required to initiate a change. Every man has own abilities and skills and when we put those together--we should not be lacking in any area. We should have businesses for our communities. We should be offering services and solutions in our communities. We should be at the forefront of change and impactful initiatives in our local communities. As one strong body of men, we can be a powerful weapon of empowerment and encouragement.

Leaders know which direction to lead their people and our direction is forward. The African American culture has been behind for many years and it is going to take more than the efforts of our political leaders to progress forward. In the past, our men stepped up to the plate and did not wait on the government. As men, we should channel that energy that our forefathers had before us. We must study our history and pick up the torch, take charge, and finish the journey that our ancestors started.

We are winners; the victory is ours, but to claim it, every man must be accountable and step up to the occasion. When one of us is down and weak, we must look to him, pick him up, and declare to him, "Be Strong, my Brotha," because brighter days are over the horizon.

ACKNOWLEDGEMENTS

First and foremost, I want to thank God for blessing me with the strength and courage to write this book. The journey has not been easy by far. When I initially started writing, my MacBook computer blacked out and I was devastated and slightly defeated. My computer crashing took away some of my motivation and I put the book on the back burner. After some long months of delay and redetermination, I retrieved my beginning work from Google Drive and continued writing and pushed through the difficult times to complete this book.

Thank you to all the men that I have encountered throughout my life who have shared substantial knowledge and wisdom, thus developing my leadership and abilities. From studying influential, inspirational speakers such as Les Brown and Eric Thomas to learning from pastors such as Dr. Myles Munroe and Bishop T.D. Jakes, I've had the opportunity to grow and transform into the righteous man that I am today. From infant days to adulthood, I have been blessed to have some phenomenal men in my personal life. My father, grandfather, and uncles all have played a major part and my desire to write this book and inspire every man in my connections. There are also a few of my college professors whom I believe would be proud to know I challenged myself to write this book.

Thank you to my family, and all my friends who listened to my provisional ideas and received small excerpts over the course of this process. Without all your support, it would not have been possible. You guys are truly rock stars and I am so grateful that you have been patient with me.

Thank you to my colleagues of S & J Empowers who inspired me to put my words into this book and encouraging me to improve and increase my writing abilities. You guys have been my accountability partners that ensured I stayed committed to finishing this project after the crashing of my computer. I am grateful to be a part of this company and look forward to the future.

ABOUT THE AUTHOR

Damien O. Jefferson, devoted father, son, friend, is an author, motivational speaker, fitness enthusiast, and Youth Leadership and Life Coach with a mission to influence and impact the next generation of greatness. Damien has experienced his fair share of trials and tribulations and he has used them all to step into his purpose in life.

Damien has a divine passion for serving and empowering the youth to grow and develop into the future leaders of tomorrow. He believes in bridging the gap between the younger generation and the old so that everyone can be successful and live prosperous lives.

Damien is also the Creative Director of S & J Empowers, empowerment consulting company, and a Co-host of the S & J Uncensored Podcast. Through these channels, he can deliver his experience and wisdom to everyone who is aspiring to create a legacy.

Made in the USA
San Bernardino, CA
04 March 2020